AF333964

IN PURSUIT OF
EXTREME GREATNESS

AN ER DOCTOR AND ULTRAMARATHONER'S
PRESCRIPTION FOR ELEVATING
YOUR LIFE BEYOND LIMITS

IN PURSUIT OF EXTREME GREATNESS

DR. RUSS REINBOLT

Published and distributed by Merack Publishing
San Diego, USA
www.merackpublishing.com

Library of Congress Control Number: 2023923016

Reinbolt, Russ
In Pursuit of Extreme Greatness: An ER Doctor and Ultramarathoner's Prescription for Elevating Your Life Beyond Limits

ISBN: 978-1-957048-93-2 Paperback
ISBN: 978-1-949635-23-2 eBook
ISBN: 978-1-957048-06-2 Hardcover

This book is dedicated to my daughters, Ella and Erica—my love for you angels cannot be put into words—and to my wife, Diane, who has been with me every step, but also to every patient I've ever seen, as you've made my journey what it is.

CONTENTS

"Ultramarathons, or ultras, are any running races beyond the standard marathon distance of 26.2 miles (or 42.2k). The most common ultra distances are 50k, 100k, 50 miles, or 100 miles, but each event is unique in terms of distance and terrain.

The International Association of Athletics Federation recognises world records at ultramarathon events that have a distance of 100km. There are even 24hr ultramarathons, where the distance is unlimited, or multi day ultras, where the distance can extend beyond 1000km.

There are a couple of city-based ultramarathons, but most ultras make the most of the USA's stunning scenery and landscapes. A lot of these events go off-road and require trail-running over difficult terrain with steep climbs or along rugged coastlines. There are over 1,500 ultramarathon events in the USA.

One of the most famous and most difficult events is the Badwater Ultramarathon, which is 135 miles long through the searing heat and arduous terrain of Death Valley."

www.letsdothis.com[1]

---

1 "Ultramarathons in the USA," letsdothis.com, https://www.letsdothis.com/us/running-events/ultramarathon.

HOW IT ALL STARTED

The importance of striving for lifelong continuous growth and improvement is hard to overestimate.

I didn't complete a 430-mile ultramarathon in the Arctic just by showing up at the starting line. I built my way progressively. First, I had to make a choice to run, and for me, that journey began when I was a skinny teenager. Over the years, I took on longer and harder races, setting new goals for myself.

But, let's not get ahead of ourselves. We need to start at the beginning.

"No, Mom. I don't want to wear that shirt," I said, wrinkling my nose with distaste at the tank top she held up. She knew why.

I didn't want to wear the shirt because I thought it showed my skinny, wimpy arms. It was late summer before my freshman year of high school. All my friends were getting taller and more "muscley." I wasn't. Easily the shortest kid in my class at barely five feet tall, I fit the bill of a ninety-five-pound weakling. I had no self-confidence. Most boys grow taller first, then "fill out." I didn't do either until I started lifting weights in the basement of our home a few years later.

I didn't look it, but I was still pretty strong for my size. In eighth grade, I came two reps short of beating the school record for chin-ups. That was a small consolation. All I cared about was my appearance—and I thought everyone saw me as a toothpick.

To make matters worse, despite being an outstanding baseball and basketball player until then, I got cut from tryouts for both sports the previous year. I was too small. I had played catcher, believe it or not, even though I was considered a pip-squeak.

It got to the point where I couldn't throw anybody out stealing second or even third base. In one game, the opposite team's coach told every player who got on base to steal on me. I was publicly humiliated.

"Take off. Russ can't throw it that far," he shouted at his team in earshot of everyone else.

My family could tell I was having confidence issues. Thank God for my big brother.

"Why don't you try out for the cross-country team?" he asked me one day.

I had started running a two-mile loop, inspired by the father of one of my classmates who ran past our house in northwestern Ohio several times per week. I usually saw him when I was outside mowing the lawn.

I did pretty well, never really getting tired and moving at a good clip. I thought, "What the heck? I might as well try it. My ball sports career is over already!"

I started doing my two-mile loop twice. Then three times. Then four times. I kept a log of my workouts. My Mom bought me real running shoes, and I started getting into the sport. I couldn't wait for the first practice.

It came. I think I was the first kid to show up. Then some juniors and seniors showed up. I couldn't have been more intimidated. The head coach arrived, introduced himself, and told us what to expect in the first few weeks. We would run a six-miler that day—three miles to just over the Michigan state line, turn around, and head back the same way.

Ten minutes in, I somehow was in second place! Either the other guys weren't in shape yet, or I was on to something here. When I arrived back at the school, the coach told me I did a great job. I was hooked.

Everyone experiences defining moments in their lives. I had no idea how profound this one would be. I can't imagine my life without it including running. Now fifty-eight years old, I have been running almost continually since. I've done countless triathlons, road races, and trail races from 5K jaunts up to 330 miles in backwoods Alaska, including five Badwater Ultras in the heat of Death Valley, six 200-mile races, 300 miles in Swedish Lapland, and a 430-mile race in The Yukon.

Running directed me into a life of health and wellness that has been shared actively and passively with countless others. It set the groundwork for my interest in the human body, culminating in a career in medicine.

It also set me on a relentless pursuit to achieve Extreme Greatness in many aspects of my life—from the ER to the backcountry forests I run through. No matter the context, every time I worked hard to achieve a goal, there was a moment of celebration followed by an immediate drive to level up. This constant desire to be better and push the boundaries of my capabilities has followed me since adolescence.

Thanks, Big Bro Jake!! It's all your fault.

INTRODUCTION

In ultramarathons, I have experienced the lowest of lows—thinking death was near—while later in the same race being in absolute utopia. When alone for days in punishing environments, the sense of doom and horrific despair can be overwhelming. Ultramarathoners can tolerate the highest level of physical and emotional suffering—I think more than any athlete. As a result, we have a wonderful perspective on life in general.

As an emergency doctor, I've seen great misery (telling a family of the death of a loved one or delivering a terminal cancer diagnosis) while alternatively witnessing the other end of the spectrum of elation and maximal happiness (telling a family I saved their loved one's life or after delivering a baby).

I've spent the majority of my adult life chasing my maximum potential—both professionally and personally. What I do is not crazy. It is extreme. My goal has always been to be great. My ultimate goal, therefore, is to achieve Extreme Greatness.

LIFE IS AN ULTRAMARATHON

Ultramarathons have taught me many lessons that I have been able to apply to other aspects of my life. In running (and in life), you make a decision to set a goal, and then you need to come up with a plan to achieve it. Next, you have to execute, which sometimes takes enormous sacrifice—personal, financial, and otherwise. A goal often changes your priorities because you are remaining focused on what really matters.

And then, there is the moment of reward, which can barely be put into words. Once you reach a point in your life when you have achieved something, when you can use that achievement to teach, inspire, and help others, *that's* Extreme Greatness. The pursuit of using your sacrifice and drive to become a leader is a life-changing process. It alters you in a way that is almost always for the better.

FROM THE BACKCOUNTRY ROADS TO THE EMERGENCY ROOM

My journey to becoming a doctor was not so different from my decision to compete in ultramarathons. I would go so far as to say it is analogous to the greatest degree.

College, medical school, residency…it's an ultramarathon in education and experience. And the sacrifice is steep. There

were so many times I wanted to throw my books away. I was sick of studying! But I kept at it. I didn't give up on my dream.

The difference is, in medicine there is no finish line. Even when you retire, you will always be inclined to help others. It's a lifelong calling toward greatness, a continuous road to becoming the best you can possibly be.

I would suggest, though, that life—and the pursuit of Extreme Greatness—also has no finish line. It's not a box you can check, *"Done! I have officially achieved Extreme Greatness. Now I can rest."*

It is a continual pursuit of personal evolution.

GRATITUDE AND SERVICE

When you are on a lifelong journey, you need to periodically stop and smell the roses, so to speak. It is really important to look back and assess your progress, to soak in the gratification of how far you have come. Even if you have not reached your goal *yet,* you can probably stop and say, *"Look what I've done already. I'm a changed person."* It will fuel you and motivate you to keep going.

You can't always be striving, striving, striving. There is value in taking a pause, acknowledging your blessings, and asking how you can use your wisdom and good fortune to raise others alongside you.

I believe service and gratitude are key components in the pursuit of Extreme Greatness.

Altruism, or living a life of service to others, is not only the right thing to do but it defines who I am. Helping people in any manner possible and whenever possible, especially those who aren't able to help themselves, has become a driving force in my reality.

A few years ago, I came to realize all the wonderful blessings truly and deeply in my life. I have experienced painful losses, heartbreaks, and setbacks, like all others. But these negatives have been overwhelmed by good and positivity. Not a day goes by when I don't thank God for his grace to me. When one has a mindset of gratitude and service, it is impossible to be negative and unhappy, clearing the path to Extreme Greatness.

I look at altruism and gratitude as the fuel that drives my engine. You should too.

P2D2: THE FOUR PILLARS THAT UNDERLIE EXTREME GREATNESS

My life has been a wild roller coaster ride, and I've learned many lessons. For years people have been telling me, "Russ, you should write a book!" I'm a storyteller at heart, so it seemed natural to put my compelling experiences on paper and share them with you. Before sitting down to write, I thought long and hard about how I could make the most powerful impact, what it was *exactly* that I wanted to say. I wondered what Extreme Greatness was made of. After many hours of contemplation, I was able to distill my thoughts into four distinct pillars of Extreme Greatness.

These pillars form the foundation of everything I want to share with you.

- Patience
- Persistence
- Dedication
- Discipline

PATIENCE

pa·tience

/ˈpāSH(ə)ns/

noun

the capacity to accept or tolerate delay, trouble, or suffering without getting angry or upset[2]

The process of obtaining a goal can be lengthy. Many people grow weary and often quit the pursuit. When starting, individuals must realize it will take time, perhaps a very long time, to achieve their wildest dreams. Nowadays, few are able to delay gratification. They want instant satisfaction. Those who are truly *great* realize there are no substitutes for true patience. Sometimes one can hurry things up, but most of the time, things proceed beyond our control (like being in a highway traffic jam!), and we can't do a damn thing about it.

As my patience has been constantly tested over the years, through focus and continual practice I have developed this virtue into one of my best strengths.

I am often asked, "How do I become patient?" Well, it's much easier than most people think.

A few years ago, I had an "Aha moment." I needed three things to be completed immediately, and there was absolutely nothing I could do about any of them. Like a gift from God, I told myself to just completely let go of everything. I realized that by letting go, I actually was in control. I had reached a point of inner peace, liberating me from any mental unrest. Shortly thereafter, I reread the familiar Serenity Prayer, which put the process into words perfectly:

"God grant me the serenity to accept the things I cannot change, the courage to change the things I can, and the wisdom to know the difference…"

In my ultramarathons, I have no choice but to endure days (not minutes or hours) of seemingly never-ending solitude, as well as physical and emotional desperation. I cannot speed up time. I can, however, speed up my *perception* of time.

My Mental Skills Coach in San Diego, Brian Alexander, taught me to emphasize the power of living in the moment. This prevents the negative mindset that comes from dreading the magnitude of a gigantic task. Of course, we have to prepare for the time ahead; but, most importantly, dealing with the time at hand is a very powerful tool. "Chunk it down," he told me. This means, take the race and break it down into smaller and smaller sections. Try to win each moment. Over time, they will add up to a successful outcome. Since applying this, I have thrived. I'm sure you will too.

PERSISTENCE

per·sist·ence

/pərˈsistəns/

noun

firm or obstinate continuance in a course of action in spite of difficulty or opposition[2]

Have I ever been tempted to give up? Hell yes! So many times! The mental grind of focusing on the big picture instead of becoming overwhelmed by a difficult moment cannot be underestimated. I have run until my legs gave out from under me. I have stared at medical textbooks until my eyes were so blurry I could no longer see. I have questioned if the sacrifice was worth it.

What kept me going? The mantra that I want to live a *great* life, not just a mediocre one.

I'm not going to sugarcoat this for you. The pursuit of Extreme Greatness is not an easy one. It will break you down, then build you back up to become stronger, wiser, more badass. It's important to surround yourself with people who understand your journey and may even share the desire for personal evolution. Creating a community that will lift you up when you are down is an incredible benefit. No one can do this alone. In the ER, I work with a team of dedicated doctors and nurses who not only save lives together, but they share moments of despair and stories of triumph. In ultramarathons, I am profoundly grateful for the team of people who care for me—both emotionally and physically—when I am in the midst of a race.

When times get tough, when I feel like giving up, people around me stoke the fires of my persistence and remind me to carry on.

DEDICATION

ded·i·ca·tion

/ˌdedəˈkāSH(ə)n/

noun

**the quality of being dedicated or
committed to a task or purpose[2]**

In the emergency room, I am extremely dedicated to providing the best care possible to patients and families. This drive requires me to continually learn and improve. It robs me of sleep, regular meals, and time with my family. It requires me to collaborate, consult, and defer to those who have more expertise. All of this sacrifice is worth the effort if it means I can save a life, or provide comfort to someone in the worst moments imaginable.

In the sport of ultramarathon, the sacrifices are not that different than in medicine, and the dedication needed is equally immense. This sport takes time, fortitude, steadiness, incredible effort, money, and the ability to embrace pain as a tool to make me stronger. Again, my dedication is unquestionably rewarded each time I cross a finish line.

Dedication is all about return on investment (ROI). There is a cost to every choice you make. Even the choice of *not* pursuing your goal has a price tag. You need to weigh the risk, the cost, and the reward, and then make your decision accordingly.

DISCIPLINE

dis·ci·pline

/ˈdisəplən/

noun

the practice of training people to obey rules or a code of behavior, using punishment to correct disobedience[2]

As a doctor, I am extremely disciplined. It takes tremendous restraint to say what needs to be said and to know what shouldn't be said. I treat patients I don't want to see. I have to deliver bad news. I have to stay up all night and work into the

---

2 *Oxford Language Dictionary,* Oxford Languages, Oxford University Press, 2023, https://languages.oup.com/dictionaries.

wee hours of the morning. I have to remain calm in the most stressful of moments.

As an athlete, I create a detailed training regimen and stick to it, even on days when running is the last thing I want to do. Quitting, even for a day, is a slippery slope—it affects the quality of the outcome I am working toward. So, I hit the gym, eat nutritiously, and pound the pavement hour after hour in the snow, the rain, the wind, and the hail. I run in the dark and in solitude. It gets lonely. It's grueling. And I do it anyway because discipline is what makes me tough. My hard work carries me to the finish line.

Though I am not a robot, I try to be as emotionless as possible. It may seem heartless, but I have learned that emotions just complicate all situations. At times, everyone feels sad, angry, guilty, anxious, etc. As a thinking and feeling human being with a brain, it is important to recognize the role emotions play in our lives. But they very often lead to our downfall. Our words, decisions, and actions should be driven by logical, rational thought and adulterated discipline.

When one makes decisions based on emotions, bad things usually happen. We all have seen the problems that occur when people lose control of their impulses, which are grounded in…emotions. I see this day in and day out in the emergency room. I've also seen it in races.

I feel strongly that the pursuit of Extreme Greatness requires that emotions be taken out of the process. You need to be calculating, focused, and steadfast to keep pushing yourself past barriers you thought impossible to break. Emotions—fear, doubt, frustration, exhaustion—will keep you from smashing through. That is why discipline is one of the essential Pillars of Greatness.

WHY P2D2?

Patience, persistence, dedication, and discipline (P2D2) are the ingredients that have led to my version of Extreme Greatness. Without these grounding pillars, I would have sought shortcuts. I would find myself searching for the fastest, easiest way to get the job done. I would avoid roadblocks and obstacles. In essence, I would have missed so many opportunities to grow and become better.

P2D2 reminds me to live the *right* way (which is often the harder way). Why embrace the hard? Because it is the *only* way to become truly great.

Why chase greatness? Quite simply, greatness, or just the pursuit of it, enriches our lives and of everyone around us. As we continue to celebrate successes, we can inspire others to make the conscious decision to improve their own lives.

The skeptic might ask, "What is wrong with being average or just living an ordinary life?" My answer: Nothing. It's hard being great, and not everyone wants it. In truth, this book is not for those who are satisfied with being average. My hunch is, though, that the very fact you were drawn to open this book is proof that you are not okay with mediocrity. You likely have the spark of greatness simmering within you.

I want you to be great. You *can* be great. Everyone can. But only you will define what that will be…for you. It might consist of being a better version of yourself tomorrow than you are today. It might just be achieving a solitary goal. Basically, it just means improvement in one or all aspects of your life.

I know it sounds cliché, but I like helping people. I want to help you. I will teach you how to use the P2D2 pillars to transform yourself into a person of Extreme Greatness.

This book is filled with compelling stories from my life as an ultramarathon athlete and emergency room doctor that exemplify each pillar. Even if you are not an ultramarathoner or extreme athlete, I know this book can inspire you. You see, it's not about the running. It's about the lessons the running taught me.

Most of us have an area (or multiple areas) in our lives that we want to improve, where we want to stretch out our hands and reach for greatness. If that last sentence resonates, this book is for you.

Along with the stories of my adventures, I will share tips and tricks for cultivating P2D2 in your own life. I hope that by reading my story, you can begin to intentionally craft your own epic autobiography.

There are no shortcuts—athlete or not—but I can definitely point you down the path of cultivating Extreme Greatness.

ARE YOU READY TO CHOOSE EXTREME GREATNESS?

Becoming great requires you to get out of your head and spring into action. Pursuing personal growth is not a passive decision. Improvement is empowering, but it requires an insatiable hunger.

You might be thinking that this seems intimidating. While it is normal to feel nervous at the beginning of a life-changing quest, I challenge you by asking, *What is the cost of settling?*

Regret.

I don't want you to look back on your life and wish you had done more, tried harder, helped more people. The pain of regret lasts forever. Missed opportunities will haunt you for the rest of your life. This book is the antidote to regret.

In reading this book, I want you to feel like you can take on the world. I want you to feel invincible, like you can accomplish anything you set your mind to. I want to motivate you, inspire you, and help you maximize your potential. When you finish reading, I want you to put the book down and pound your chest like a gorilla. But my greatest hope is that you harness this incredible rush of emotion and turn it into action.

Just as one cannot wake up one day and decide to do an ultramarathon without the arduous training, Extreme Greatness is not achieved in a day. Or two. Or a hundred. When you put this book down, I urge you to begin making small, incremental changes. Get up fifteen minutes early each morning to exercise or meditate. Take the stairs instead of the elevator. Cook a healthy meal instead of stopping for fast food on the way home. Each little choice you make serves to empower your progress. After committing to small choices made day after day, you will begin to see the results of your sacrifice. Talk is cheap. You need to start executing and living according to P2D2.

I wrote this book for those who want to be great. I wrote it for YOU!

Because I want you to take the lessons I've learned and use them to inspire your own personal evolution, I've included an "Extreme Greatness Challenge" at the end of each chapter. They are simply questions to reflect on or quick activities to try. You may be inclined to skip over this section of the book, and in truth, it won't hinder your comprehension. However, I encourage you to push back against any resistance you might have. After all, in your quest to attain Extreme Greatness, do you *really* think you can cut corners?

So, here we go. It is time to dive in headfirst. Stop thinking. Stop talking. Let's get this S#!T done!

CHAPTER 1

THE IMPORTANCE OF SETTING GOALS

"My goal is not to be better than anyone else, but to be better than I used to be."

–WAYNE DYER

We all know those people. I'm talking about the ones who have an inner confidence that projects strength, security, and non-offensive "swagger."

I think that swagger is the result of two distinct traits: self-assuredness and positivity.

Some just "have it." For others, self-assuredness and positivity can be developed over time, resulting from incremental growth and development. This can be cultivated by goal setting.

Before a game, professional athletes tell themselves they WILL win. Of course, they have a 50% chance, but their positive mindset is essential.

In business sales, one must have self-assuredness that supports success. People should silently tell themselves, "I WILL MAKE THIS DEAL!"

Individuals who possess these traits project a power that one can feel as soon as they enter a room. Emergency doctors bring calm to stressful circumstances because we have tremendous confidence in our abilities. I sure wasn't this way early in my career. But with training and experience, my self-assuredness grew, knowing I could save anybody's life. Of course, that's not reality, but we doctors tell ourselves that. Sometimes we're called cocky. I don't mind that, though. What we have is the strongest possible belief in ourselves because we *have* to. A second of doubt can lead to catastrophe.

I embrace this same mindset when I sign up for an ultramarathon. I think positively and get excited about the challenge that lies ahead because I know I have the skills to conquer the path I am about to embark on.

Each race I sign up for, each medical emergency I avert, each goal I set, helps me grow. I celebrated smaller wins at first, then as I gained confidence and "swagger," I reached for progressively larger goals. Before long, I developed a sense of invincibility and power that could deliver Extreme Greatness.

THE SECRET WEAPON OF GOAL-SETTING

I have many "Secret Weapons." One of these: I set goals. It is a simple yet amazingly powerful growth technique. Setting goals—huge or small—can yield great results.

Goal-setting can be tremendously motivating. In fact, research shows that goal-setting drives us in a number of ways:

1. It directs our attention to what is important and away from activities irrelevant to our goal.
2. It increases our confidence as we discover and master task-relevant knowledge and strategies.
3. It reminds us that we "have the power to actively control [our] lives through purposeful thought."[3]

I look at incremental goals as stepping stones on the path to Extreme Greatness. Reaching a lofty goal can be so intimidating that one never makes the first move! So…just start small.

Experts advise that while "long-term goals provide direction for performance enhanced efforts, short-term goals serve as intermediate steps necessary for reaching [those] long-term goals and should provide more opportunities to achieve performance standards to enhance on-going motivation and confidence."[4]

Here's a silly example: Suppose someone wants to work on their abs. I would tell him or her to set a goal of doing a plank exercise for two minutes. But to make it, one would have to break the big goal down into smaller goals. Start at

---

3   Edwin A. Locke, "Building a practically useful theory of goal setting and task motivation: A 35-year odyssey," (The American Psychologist, 2002, Volume: 57, Issue: 9, Page: 705-717).

4   Zeljika Vidic & Damon Burton, "The Roadmap: Examining the Impact of a Systematic Goal-Setting Program for Collegiate Women's Tennis Players,"(The Sport Psychologist, 2010, Volume 24: Issue 4).

thirty seconds. Then each day, add fifteen seconds. In less than a week, the target of two minutes will be reached. Reaching a goal delivers wonderful satisfaction. This satisfaction is a force multiplier of motivation. They both feed each other. This principle can be applied in academics, a home project, one's career advancement, personal growth, athletic competition, and, of course, fitness and health.

And, bonus... Achievement goals cultivate overall life satisfaction! Successfully reaching your goals can positively contribute to your happiness.[5] So, what's stopping you?

The bottom line: TAKE THAT FIRST STEP!

SETTING "EXTREME" GOALS

One research article explained that "it takes a strong will, great belief and perhaps a thick skin to persevere especially if all around you are less than encouraging or supportive. There are many elements which keep us on track: determination, self-belief, conviction, wanting to prove the opposition wrong, the will to succeed, a competitive streak and sheer bloody-mindedness may all play a part. And more often than not

---

5   Wang W, Li J, Sun G, Cheng Z, Zhang XA, "Achievement goals and life satisfaction: the mediating role of perception of successful agency and the moderating role of emotion reappraisal," (Psicol Reflex Crit, 2017, Dec 22; 30(1):25).

when we succeed, the feeling is all the sweeter if we can prove the dissenters wrong."[6]

I think we need to acknowledge that while each of us has likely curated our individual vision of success (financial, relationship, career, athletic, etc.), extreme goal-setting is not for the faint of heart. The research I cited above reminded me of a term coined by journalist and writer Malcolm Gladwell: *outliers*. According to Gladwell, *outliers* "are people who do not fit into our normal understanding of achievement…they are exceptional people…those who operate at the extreme outer edge of what is statistically plausible."[7]

These seem like my kind of people—those who chase Extreme Greatness.

SETTING YOURSELF UP FOR SUCCESS

Whether your goal is audacious or plays on a smaller field, having strategies and a plan increase your chances of success. My next dive into research was a quest to discover just that: how can we increase our chances of actually attaining the goals we set?

According to Angela Lee Duckworth (whose research on "grit" has become globally renowned), while the "goal-setting phase"

---

6   Rachel Busuttil Leaver, "Achieving greatness–nature, nurture, or just plain luck?" (The International Journal of Urological Nursing, 2012, Feb 20, https://doi.org).

7   https://en.wikipedia.org/wiki/Outliers_(book)

gets the ball rolling, the crux of a person's success occurs in the "goal-striving phase." She advocates for a strategy termed *"mental contrasting"* where one conjures "contrasting fantasies about a desired future with reflections about obstacles that prevent their realization. [Basically, the individual will create a] mental elaboration of the desired future and the present reality, thereby making both simultaneously accessible and creating strong associations between them. In mental contrasting, the positive future is elaborated first, and the negative reality is framed as 'standing in the way' of realizing the positive future. The simultaneous activation of the desired future and present reality emphasizes the necessity for action. When expectations of success are high, mental contrasting energizes individuals to take action and strengthens their goal commitment."[8]

Layman's terms? Picture the life you have now. Then, picture the life you want (which includes the achievement of your goal). Decide which version you would rather have—most of us will choose excellence over the mundane—and then make a plan to get there.

Another strategy I came across came from the website mindtools.com. They call it "SMART goals"[9]:

---

8   A.L. Duckworth, H. Grant, B. Loew, G. Oettingen, & P. M. Gollwitzer, "Self-regulation strategies improve self-discipline in adolescents: Benefits of mental contrasting and implementation intentions," (Educational Psychology, 2011, 31(1), 17–26, https://doi.org/10.1080/01443410.2010.506003).

9   https://www.mindtools.com/a4wo118/smart-goals

S - specific

M - measurable

A - achievable

R - relevant

T - time bound

What I appreciate about this strategy is that it takes your goal out of the ether and grounds it in an action plan.

When I decided I wanted to become a doctor, I…

- (S) set my sights on being accepted into medical school
- (M) measured success on a) my acceptance and b) my GPA
- (A) knew if I followed the prescribed path, I would graduate into residency
- (R) chose this path to make a positive impact on the world
- (T) researched exactly how many years my education would take

When I sign up for an ultramarathon, I…

- (S) have a specific distance I need to train for
- (M) create a plan that outlines how many miles I need to run each week
- (A) know that if I stick to my training plan, my chances of crossing the finish line are pretty good

- (R) know that running ultras moves me forward on my quest for Extreme Greatness
- (T) write the date of the race on my calendar and curate my training plan backward from there.

GOAL-SETTING AND THE PILLARS OF EXTREME GREATNESS

I rely upon the P2D2 Pillars as the foundation for my existence in everyday life. But when it comes to setting a goal, they become even more important.

In the journey to reach a goal, there will be times when each Pillar will be relied upon in different amounts. For example, it will not take a great amount of *patience* to accomplish a small goal, but it may take tremendous *discipline*. Discipline is a muscle I am continuously working to build, even in the smallest, silliest of ways. One exercise I do to build discipline and toughness is if I get an itch somewhere, like on my nose or something, or if a fly lands on me, I try not to scratch it. I know that sensation is going to go away eventually, but the discipline it takes not to address it is harder than it sounds!

Depending on the difficulty of the challenge or the length of the goal, I will rely upon the Pillars to different degrees. Smaller goals and daily practices of the Pillars will prepare you to take on larger, more exciting challenges.

When setting a long-term goal, the Pillars become even more important. Let's say somebody is a senior in high school, and they've made the decision they want to become a doctor or a lawyer—a career that requires not just a bachelor's degree but a graduate-level degree. Or maybe someone wants to build a house as an investment, which is a long, multi-step process. The greater the goal, the greater the reliance on the Pillars for a longer period of time and to a greater depth.

That's not going to be easy. There will be setbacks along the way. Some can be crushing and seemingly fatal, which might completely derail a process or a project. In those really tough moments, you need to embrace the Pillars and remind yourself that it's okay to lose some battles, but you don't wanna lose the war.

Those bigger goals are meant to stretch you and require sacrifice, but they offer a greater reward.

TAKE A PAUSE

I'm big on reflection, especially when I find myself in the thick of it. I'm very introspective and intentionally steal little moments to myself where I can dive right into my head. Sometimes I see a bee flying over a flower and take a minute to just stare at it. I think about how grateful I am to be in a position where I can chase extreme goals. There are times in my day, particularly when I'm running, when I have such amazing clarity of thought that I can prioritize things and put them in what I consider appropriate perspective.

Whether you are a deep thinker, write in a journal, practice mindfulness, or find time for meditation, I highly recommend the tool of reflection. It keeps me going forward chasing greatness but also forces a pause where I can evaluate the process I am embarking on. You don't want to be go, go, go all the time.

Take the Marines, for example. When attacking an enemy, they don't just go all in, all at once. They advance, they stop, they check everything, they get new intelligence, then advance again. Stop, reflect, do things in stages.

It's the same philosophy when you are pursuing a goal. You have to stop once in a while. You can't just be hell-bent, thinking *I'm gonna make it, I'm gonna make it, I'm gonna make it.* I know it's not sexy to stop and check in on your plan and reassess the Pillars. But it is something that I consider to be essential.

The same mentality applies in the busy emergency department. We get small bits of information that change our strategy tremendously. A patient may come in by ambulance with an altered level of consciousness. We don't know if the problem is drug ingestion, a poisoning, or maybe sepsis—an infection taken over their body. We don't know if it's a metabolic disturbance from something like diabetes. It can be all types of things.

The first measure is to try and resuscitate them without knowing exactly what's going on. Then, as information becomes available, we reassess and redirect. We might start therapy or prescribe a certain treatment and then see how the patient responds. Based on that response, we make another advancement, just like the Marines. Charge, pause, charge, pause.

With regards to chasing a goal, you advance and then you check in to see how you are doing. If a certain pursuit or path is not working, then it is time to go down a different direction.

In ultramarathon, there are times when you can run very fast and chew up the miles. You might consider, *This is a flat section. I can run this very fast.* But then there are times—like climbing a mountain on technical terrain—when you have to go very slowly. If you try to attack it and go too fast, or be too aggressive, it can be counterproductive. You can twist an ankle or burn valuable energy.

In pursuing an extreme goal, you need to be strategic and be willing to pivot. You need to plan, pause, reflect, and adjust. All of these qualities rely heavily on patience, persistence, dedication, and discipline, and the combination will keep you on the road to success.

EXTREME GREATNESS CHALLENGE:

Write down or think about your personal definition of success. What areas of your life need accolades, challenges, and/or growth in order for you to feel successful?

Write down your bucket list of audacious goals. Do they correlate with your definition of success?

Choose one of those goals and create a plan using the SMART goal strategy.

CHAPTER 2

EMBRACING DISCOMFORT

"I'm not crazy... I'm just not you."

–DAVID GOGGINS

The road to greatness is never easy, but I believe discomfort is the birthplace of growth. If we didn't struggle, if we were always comfortable, we'd never change.

The sport I've chosen is the greatest metaphor for the idea of embracing challenges that I could ever imagine.

I have never heard another ultrarunner give a concise, brief, and understandable explanation for why we do what we do. There are innumerable reasons we do events that seem like true torture to others. I've thought about my "why" a lot. I've come to understand that through running, I'm seeking my ultimate state of contentment. Reaching that state requires a four-step process:

1. Setting a goal, which is the easiest.
2. Training and planning, which is my favorite. For me, I get immense satisfaction from "the chase."
3. Discipline and Accountability.
4. Executing. This is the hardest part.

In addition, I enjoy being out in rough wilderness conditions alone and having to rely on my mental and physical fortitude to reach always-expanding self-defined limits. As the Navy SEALs say, "Embrace the Suck."

Once again, it comes down to extremes. The greater the pain, the greater the pleasure when the pain stops.

We're all human beings. We each have a different makeup of character and background, but we all have struggles. Some people self-impose destructive cycles like addiction, illogical decision-making, and making bad choices. Others of us choose constructive struggles as opportunities for growth and self-realization and to strengthen ourselves. I want you to choose the latter.

In my desire to normalize discomfort for you, I will spend this chapter sharing some of my primary struggles.

STRUGGLE #1.

I get asked a lot of questions. It comes with the territory of being an ultramarathon runner, especially one who does the most extreme events. Let's face it. We're a rare breed. The word "crazy" gets thrown my way routinely. It used to bother me. Now it empowers me.

To borrow a quote from perhaps the most well-known ultra-athlete out there, David Goggins: "I'm not crazy…I'm just not you." I can't state it any better than he does.

Perhaps my greatest struggle is my inability to give a solid answer when someone asks me, "Russ, why do you do those crazy events?" Well…it's complicated!

When will I be completely content? From an athletic standpoint, that state will arrive when I don't have any regrets involving my journey to reach my perceived highest degree of Extreme Greatness. When I'm in my last days, I'll sit in a rocking chair overlooking the beach and say, "I gave it my all."

And also, as a patient once told me, "God was good to me."

STRUGGLE #2.

Professionally, I want to be known and respected as an excellent emergency physician. I'm confident most people see me that way. I suppose patients take something positive from hearing about my non-doctor life. That is great, but it isn't what I want to matter. When I'm in the emergency department, it's all about the patient, NOT me.

I know sometimes I inspire others to seek personal growth and improvement. I'll take that attention every day. I also know some people think I do ultras to impress others. No way. If I wanted that, I would choose a much easier path!

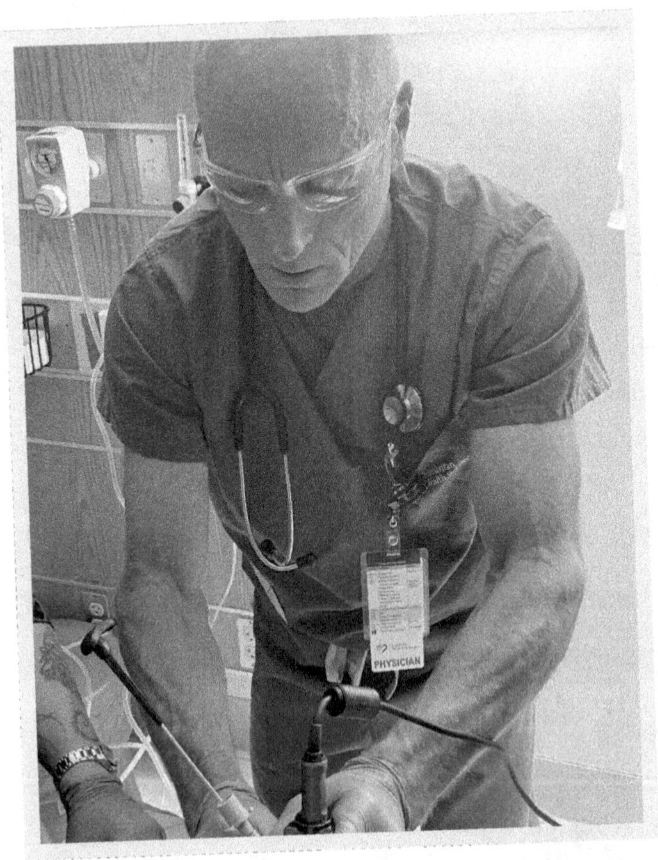

But by doing events at the outermost limits of people's imaginations, my alter-ego sometimes overshadows my doctoring. I can't say how many times I've been engaged in a discussion of an exciting medical case at a packed table in the doctors' dining room when the talk switches to my ultralife.

"When is your next race, Russ?"

"How's your training going?"

I'm surrounded by some of the smartest people in the world, for whom I have the greatest respect for their intelligence and expertise. When they ask about my races, it feels like my athleticism is the source of their respect for me, not my medical knowledge.

I get it. I know they want to escape their daily grind for a few minutes. I know they're respectfully curious as well. But I don't like the focus to be on me unless it's constructive.

At work, I sometimes feel like a "fish out of water." Maybe I just need to get over it!

STRUGGLE #3.

I also struggle with expecting patients (and, for that matter, all people) to be "tougher." As a result of my years in ultras, I have developed an ability to put up with a lot of shit—both emotionally and physically. I've come to believe that we can endure levels of displeasure that simply can't be described—days of solitude, extreme hunger/cold/heat, physical pain, emotional lows that seem to never end, etc. Some of us almost pathologically crave it. A "normal" person might ask *why*?

No "normal" person enjoys pain. Through suffering, I have developed the ability to trick my mind into feeding off it, knowing the wonderful pleasure that comes when the suffering ends.

Beating the pain allows even greater satisfaction. It's a risk/reward thing. That helps explain why we keep pushing farther to things more challenging and more extreme.

I love getting famished so that when I finally eat, it tastes so much better.

I love getting super tired, so it feels much more restful when I finally sleep.

I love getting super thirsty, so it feels much more quenching when I drink.

I love setting ridiculous goals because when I accomplish them, they are more satisfying.

Fundamentally: the extremer the extreme, the greater the great! And vice versa.

So, when a patient comes in saying they're experiencing or showing signs of pain, I have to see things as a "normal" person. That's hard for me because, let's face it, I ain't! You can't be normal to do what I do, especially as a lifelong career.

I consider myself a very compassionate doctor, but often I walk away from a patient, struggling to keep from grumbling under my breath, "What a wimp!"

In conclusion, we ultrarunners sure are a different breed. Does the sport make us different, or do we go into the sport because we already are different? Interesting question. Either way, our experiences "out there" shape our thinking and interactions with others. I must always remember that patients don't see things my way many times, and they react very differently than I would in certain circumstances.

I am learning to embrace my unique strengths and not to expect them in others.

My point in sharing all of this is that my personal struggles shape my growing relationship with P2D2. The way you interpret these pillars may be different, but different is neither better nor worse. P2D2 can simply be used as a guardrail on either side of each individual journey, keeping us on a growth trajectory (however that may look).

Lastly, I want to add that while P2D2 are the pillars of Extreme Greatness, the foundation of my success was laid by the people who support me—my family, friends, and team— and from those who mentored me along the way.

I'll introduce you to them in the next chapter.

EXTREME GREATNESS CHALLENGE:

Make a list of the top two or three things you currently struggle with.

How can the P2D2 pillars help you overcome each hurdle?

CHAPTER 3

WE LEARN TO BECOME GREAT

"The delicate balance of mentoring someone is not creating them in your own image, but giving them the opportunity to create themselves."

–STEVEN SPIELBERG

Looking back on the younger versions of myself, I can't definitively say that I was born with the pillars of P2D2. They weren't innate but rather cultivated through a lifetime of learning.

I believe that learning is social as much as it is individual. While we each make our own meaning from the challenges we experience, we also need role models whom we want to emulate and who are willing to point toward the path of greatness. Mentors come in all shapes and sizes—from preschool teachers and high school coaches to leaders in the professional realm. The cool thing is, life will offer so many opportunities to learn and grow. We just need to be on the lookout for amazing teachers!

With four years of college, three years of graduate school, four years of medical school, and another four years of residency training under my belt, I can confidently say I've had innumerable (and often rather interesting) teachers over the years. This is on top of all my elementary, junior high, and high school teachers. I could write an entire book just about all of them! Some I remember vividly, but while many left their mark on me, I'm ashamed to say I can't remember all of their names.

I *do*, however, remember Miss Brandon—my kindergarten teacher at Sylvan Elementary in Sylvania. She set me off on the right path in life and reinforced the great parenting I received at home. Polite but strict, she was a model teacher and taught me about infinite patience. I wonder what she's doing now?

Mrs. Ryan, for second grade at Whiteford Elementary, laid the foundation for using proper grammar and spelling (a.k.a. discipline). Writing grew to become a hobby I still enjoy today.

Louis Levy, my high school journalism teacher, really "sealed the deal" when I was a senior. He further inspired my love for writing and the use of the English language. At the time, I didn't realize what a gift he would be to me throughout my life. As the sports editor of my high school newspaper (something I'm immensely proud of and brag to my kids about often), I had ample opportunity to refine my skills.

Funny anecdote: I'm very embarrassed and ashamed for having fallen asleep in one of his classes. He pretended to have tripped and slyly kicked my chair to wake me up. I thought it was very cool of him not to call me out in front of the entire class.

My high school geography teacher, Jeff Ustick, also coached me in track and cross country. He instilled in me a love of running and an appreciation of discipline, dedication, and persistence. Mr. Ustick was very approachable and down to earth, and I really enjoyed my time with him. I love how he pushed me hard in workouts and at track and cross-country meets.

At Michigan State, I solely focused on science classes. I hated everything else. But my humanities professor changed that. Because of him, I took an unusual liking to classical music, such as Mozart, Bach, and Beethoven. He taught me to approach new subjects, topics, and ideas with patience and reminded me not to rush to judgment.

Dr. David Lamb, the Chairman of the Exercise Physiology Department at Ohio State, served as my advisor for my Master's degree. At that time in my life, as I was obsessed with triathlons, I primarily cared about training. I must admit, academics came second. Dr. Lamb challenged me greatly, but I didn't really "get it" until after I left OSU. He was a major impetus in me pursuing more education, leading to my career in medicine. The more I learned about the human body, the more fascinated I became. He made me "hungry" for knowledge and reinforced the idea that I could be dedicated to more than one thing.

I'll never forget my Cardiology attending doctor during residency. One of the kindest and smartest souls I've ever met, this doctor made us take "breaks" every half hour or so while on patient rounds so he could go *smoke*. It took me a while to get over the fact that a Cardiologist, of all people, was a chain-smoker! Despite this oddity, the idea of breaks helped me accept their necessity for endurance (both in the hospital and when I was running). I developed an understanding that I needed to dedicate myself to the big picture, rather than just forging through the moment only to succumb to fatigue later on.

One of my Urology attending physicians had the legendary notoriety of having performed his own *vasectomy*. A cowboy boot-wearing Vietnam Veteran, he just hiked his leg up on his workbench in his garage and snip, snip, tie—and it was done! If I had been a Urologist, I probably would've done the same. A fantastic doctor and teacher, all his med students and residents loved him for his tough guy persona yet exemplary bedside manner. To be honest, I'm not sure how this story relates to P2D2, but I couldn't *not* share it with you!

I had an Orthopedist attending who hated wasting time, energy, and words. He took charge like no one I'd met before. Once, while rounding through the ER, we came upon a patient with a hip dislocation. The ER doctor described the process of "reducing" (putting it back in its socket) while preparing medications to sedate and relax the patient. It was a masterclass in his dedication to efficiency.

Among many other teachers, I'll definitely never forget my Critical Care attending, Dr. Dante Landucci. He simply, patiently, and methodically taught us the intricacies of treating the sickest of the sick in the Intensive Care Unit. I had previously been intimidated by the ICU. He took the fear away, allowing me to thrive and embrace caring for that patient population. As fate would have it, I ended up becoming an emergency physician, spending my entire career helping those with dire conditions. From him I learned it all—patience, persistence, dedication, and discipline. Thanks, Dr. Landucci, wherever you are!

I strongly believe in the *ripple effect* where one person's words or actions have an impact on others, most of whom we never know. This cycle continues over and over again, multiplying the original person's impact exponentially.

These teachers, who all became role models to me, were the ones who threw the first stone, causing those initial ripples.

I am forever grateful.

Sometimes, life presents you with mentors (as in the case of my vast education and residency). Other times, you need to seek out the right person to learn from. Either way, your job as a human being striving toward Extreme Greatness is to be a lifelong learner and actively find ways to stretch and strengthen yourself.

While the language of P2D2 came to me much later in life, I can confidently say that the seeds were sown in my youth.

All of the lessons I learned from these folks prepared me to stare down my limits—in the ER and in ultramarathon—and discover my Extreme Greatness.

I hope that by sharing some race stories, I can become one of *your* teachers, pointing you down the path toward your own potential.

EXTREME GREATNESS CHALLENGE:

Make a list of two or three people whom you consider to exemplify Extreme Greatness.

How do their actions/mindset emulate the P2D2 pillars?

What other valuable lessons have they taught you?

CHAPTER 4

WHEN THE UNEXPECTED HAPPENS

"Success is no accident. It is hard work, perseverance, learning, studying, sacrifice, and most of all, love of what you are doing or learning to do."

– PELÉ

The quest for Extreme Greatness is not a linear one. It is full of ups and downs, unexpected turns, and even some plummeting spirals. No matter what goal you are working toward, you will inevitably encounter unexpected setbacks. In these bumpy moments, your mindset will make all of the difference.

The following story, which I affectionately call "So Close Yet So Far," is meant to illustrate how P2D2 allowed me to overcome fear and stay calm in a tough situation.

At 230 miles into the Moab 240 ultramarathon, I had been having one of the best races of my life. In one of the world's toughest races, I managed all the expected problems to that point. I had dealt with the long stretches between checkpoints. I had handled both the extremely cold nighttime and blazing daytime temperatures. My hydration and nutrition needs were on point. I pushed myself to maintain a solid pace. I didn't have any injuries, and my equipment worked well. Mentally, I maintained great toughness despite the adversity of the event.

Suddenly, it all came crashing down.

As the sun set, I estimated I had around two hours before I finished the race. I checked my headlamp, and it was dead. "No problem," I said. "I'll just charge it up with my battery pack, and while it's charging up, I'll use my backup." But when I switched it on, it too was dead.

My next move: use the flashlight on my phone. Uh oh. Battery level 13%. I'm not normally afraid of anything, but this was testing me. As an ER doctor, I've had to be fearless and confident, almost cocky. Being lost in the dark was worrying me, but I knew I'd be found eventually. The problem is, the word "eventually" implies it could be a long time. I'd have to stay calm despite the situation.

As the sun approached the horizon, my angst increased. How would I see the reflective trail markers without a light source? I could see the lights of Moab far off in the distance, but that was it. Heading off the trail toward the light would be an absolute death march. There were sharp drop-offs, so going off trail would most assuredly lead to a horrible injury. And how would search and rescue get to me if needed?

I thought of grabbing some branches and making a torch. But I didn't have any matches or a way to start a fire. The temperature was dropping into the low fifties. I had about 800 calories of food and about a liter of water left.

I had one lightweight jacket in my pack but not much else, as I didn't think I would be out for a fourth night on the trail. I left everything else back at the last major checkpoint, hoping to run as light as possible.

Only a sliver of a moon presented itself, providing no light source. It couldn't have been much darker after the sunset.

I was stranded.

At one point, I saw light from a headlamp belonging to the racer ahead of me (and a few hundred feet in elevation below me). I yelled to him at the top of my lungs. He stopped but couldn't understand what I said. The anguish crushed me as he turned around and headed down the trail. I felt like I was in a lifeboat in the middle of the ocean as a rescue plane turned away after not seeing me.

My phone died rapidly, drained by the flashlight. I tried to find the next trail marker by feeling my way around and grabbing at the desert shrubs. I stopped quickly when I jabbed my hand into a giant cactus instead, penetrating my hand with at least ten painful, long needles. Without light, I delicately tried to locate them without pushing them deeper into my skin.

Now I entered full "this is a serious situation" mode. I thought of how mad my wife and girls would be at me if I died. They always tell me before I leave for a race, "Don't die, Dad." They would probably exhume my body and kill me again!!

Here I was, stranded in the desert, 230 miles into a race, exhausted after having slept only about eight hours over the last three and a half days, almost out of food and water with little clothes, no way of starting a fire, and with no way to communicate with others.

I thought of what an irresponsible fool I had been. I could either hit the SOS button on my GPS tracker, ending what was until then a fantastic race, or hunker down for the night until sunrise.

I chose the latter.

I dug a six-foot-long "foxhole" under an overlying slanted rock. I scooped out hard-packed, grainy sand with my hands. I placed my pack up on the rock, then covered myself with as much sand as possible. That would serve as my blanket for the night.

I dozed off for minutes at a time, as it was hard to fall into a deep slumber in these conditions. I thought maybe I shouldn't allow myself to go to sleep, unrealistically thinking I might freeze to death. I told myself I wouldn't be able to stay awake for the ten hours until daylight.

I prayed to the Lord Almighty above for a light source. That's all I needed—light. "Please, God, give me light." With light, I could see the markers and be on my way. That would solve all my problems.

I wracked my brain on what else I could do. Nothing came to mind. I told myself just to relax and wait things out.

After I had dozed off for several hours, my prayers were answered! Some dude yelled out, "Hey, are you in the race?" I turned over and was blinded by the headlamp of the next racer behind me. I first thought that I was dying, and this was the light people talk about when they have a near-death experience.

When I was last awake, I was in the depths of darkness. Now I was drowning in the opposite—LIGHT!

I couldn't believe the change of fortune. Within ten seconds, I had gone full circle, from one emotional extreme to the other. As an ultramarathoner and ER doctor, I live in the extreme. But this came a tad too close.

The other racer had a pacer, so now there were two headlamps. I told him how I got into this situation and how elated I was to see him. I asked if I could tuck in between them, guided by their lights down the trail.

Giddy with relief and euphoria, I couldn't contain my glee. The other two runners were so beat down that they only responded with occasional pained grunts.

One mile later, a light approached me from below. "Hey, are you Russ Reinbolt?" A race official came from the finish line to look for me. He knew I was in trouble by following my zig-zaggy tracker tracing on the computer. When the line stopped moving, he came to check on me, fearing a major problem.

Now, I had an abundance of light. What an embarrassment of riches. The official and I pulled away from the other racer and his pacer, as they were in a bad way themselves.

When I reached a road with occasional streetlights, I knew the ordeal had finally ended.

I put the hammer down and cruised the next two miles to the finish.

This experience shook me quite a bit. Being entirely out of control and not knowing what the outcome would be was tremendously unsettling.

The only way I could get control was to relinquish attempts to get it.

It worked.

The Moab race was one hell of a predicament to find myself in. The reality of my decisions hit hard, and I felt the weight of my choice to run an ultramarathon like never before. The pain and suffering I experienced that night would be nothing compared to what my family would feel if I did not make it out of that desert alive.

It would have been really easy to slide down the slippery slope of fear that night, but I made a choice to stay calm and patient while waiting for morning's light to dawn. After making the conscious decision to let go and not force action, a resolution was ultimately presented to me.

P2D2 saved me that night. My ability to fall back not only on patience but also the discipline needed to stay still and calm, the persistence to maintain a strong, positive mindset, and the dedication to my very survival helped me through the longest, darkest night of my life. Looking back, I can see how powerful that experience was.

To achieve Extreme Greatness, one must have endless tenacity and resilience to overcome unexpected (and sometimes terrifying) challenges. If the race had gone perfectly, I would have celebrated another well-deserved achievement. The fact that it was massively difficult fortified the skills that make me a better athlete and better man.

TIPS AND TRICKS FOR USING P2D2 WHEN THE UNEXPECTED OCCURS:

Patience: Understand that the goal you are working toward may take longer than anticipated to achieve. Sometimes, this makes the win even more savory.

Persistence: When you find yourself in a pause, or a moment of waiting for the next right move, don't give up. Stay still in the discomfort and wait until the right opportunity to move forward presents itself.

Dedication: Assess your priorities and keep your energy focused on what really matters.

<u>*Discipline*</u>: A strong mindset can literally save your life. Focus on the "light" within a dark situation.

EXTREME GREATNESS CHALLENGE:

Think of a time when something unexpected altered the trajectory of a goal you were trying to achieve.

Evaluate your reaction through the lens of P2D2 by giving yourself a score for each pillar:

1 - I did not exemplify this pillar.

2 - I moderately exemplified this pillar.

3 - I crushed this pillar!

If you scored any 1's, this may be an area where you can create some intentionality over the upcoming weeks. Find opportunities in your daily life to practice this pillar in moments of frustration, overwhelm, anger, or when the unexpected occurs.

CHAPTER 5

WHEN YOU DON'T CROSS THE PROVERBIAL FINISH LINE

"There are a million reasons why you can't. Focus on the few reasons why you can."

— KARA GOUCHER

The truth is, sometimes we set goals, and due to unavoidable circumstances, we don't achieve them. It can be devastating—all the time, money, and effort put forth for nothing. In your quest for Extreme Greatness, disappointment will inevitably occur. It's part of the process. In these dark moments, you can't let a minor (or major) setback derail you. You need to pick yourself up and start again. If achieving Extreme Greatness was easy, everyone would do it, wouldn't they? But then your triumphant moments wouldn't taste as sweet.

I want to preface the following story by sharing that I do not consider this race a failure. It taught me a lot about P2D2 and served to strengthen my character. As you read it, you might be reminded of a time when you fell short of your goal. I encourage you to reflect not on the "failure" itself but on the hours, days, and weeks following. How did you react? How did you reset and recover?

I call this story "Did I Not Finish Badwater?"

I had been accepted into the world-famous Badwater Ultramarathon, a grueling, iconic race in the scorching heat of the Mojave Desert of Central California. It felt like an enormous opportunity.

Two years previous, I crewed a close friend of mine while he participated and was shocked by the extreme nature of the innate suffering brought on by this race. When I first learned what my friend had signed up for, I reacted like almost everyone else does. "I could never do that race. That's crazy!"

For this 135-mile race, temperatures routinely reach 125° plus. Subsequently, it is billed as the "World's Toughest Footrace."

It's a true "hard-core" event, even by ultrarunner standards. One must build up a legit running resume to be accepted into the limited field each year.

Like most people who are exposed to Badwater, I became hooked on its allure. *I had to do it!* I was fascinated by the thought of testing myself this way. Training for it would be a considerable challenge. Then, actually doing it would be the biggest athletic feat of my life. I couldn't wait.

I did my homework and showed up at the starting line perfectly prepared. I had put in the miles, developing tremendous cardiovascular fitness. I did lots of heat training in saunas to prepare for the sweltering conditions. I completed grueling strength-training workouts and high-intensity sessions.

But there was one major problem. In the weeks leading up to the event, I experienced horrible insomnia. I couldn't get restful or adequate sleep because the details of my training and of the upcoming race kept swirling in my mind. I put too much pressure on myself. Even during the race week, I still tossed and turned at night.

Despite my restlessness, the time had come. I assembled a top-notch crew and felt that I was as ready as I was going to be. Surprisingly, the first seventy miles felt amazing, and my body performed well. Once the novelty of Badwater wore off, fatigue began to set in. I tried to take a ten-minute nap in the crew support van but, of course, didn't really fall asleep.

The lack of sleep started catching up to me as the miles progressed. Big time!

I had no choice but to start taking in more caffeine, widely used in the sport of ultras. Back then, I rarely drank coffee or caffeinated products. It had a strong effect on me.

I took a Coke or a Red Bull, which would perk me up for ten miles or so. But after that, I would have trouble keeping my eyes open. Squinting my tired eyes, I could see just enough of the white line on the left edge of the road to follow it in a zombie-like trance.

At Mile 110 (with twenty-five miles to go), I was dead in the water, and my crew didn't know how to proceed. A ten-minute cat nap in the van on the roadside failed to invigorate me, and I was in a bad way. Their solution (as advised by crew members from another team)? Give me as much caffeine as needed.

Since I had implored my team to get me to the damn finish line no matter what, they did what was suggested. I chugged down a 5-Hour Energy. Then a Rockstar. Then a Coke. I squeezed down some caffeinated gels. It worked a little bit. Finally, I took some caffeine pills. After ingesting an estimated 600 mg of caffeine, the magic kicked in and I came alive. But too much so.

Coming through one of the last checkpoints in Lone Pine, CA, I became altered. I ran great, but my mind started playing tricks on me. My head and my body didn't seem connected. I had never been like this before.

I started experiencing delusions and hallucinations and would try to correct them as I still had enough awareness to realize the visions were not real. But with each passing mile, the situation became much worse.

The hallucinations became my reality. I spoke to them out loud. I became stubborn and completely bonkers. My crew tried to orient me. With around ten miles to go, I somehow developed this delusion that I had finished the race already. Despite my wackiness, my guys pulled me forward, and I kept running. I grew to become despondent and violent—throwing elbows and finally lying down on the road and refusing to move. I was like a little child having an epic temper tantrum.

My crew had had enough. Fearing something was seriously medically wrong, they placed a stake in the side of the road to mark our spot and took me to the medical station back in town. Shockingly, I had a normal physical exam. I wasn't presenting as hyperthermic. Nothing looked wrong.

Confused, my crew put me in bed for some sleep. Finding myself in bed completely set me off. Why were they doing this? Why was I here?

When I couldn't sleep, the team tried to get me to take a bath, thinking this would fix my mental state. I couldn't process why this was happening, furthering my confusion and delusions.

Crew Captain Zack would turn the water on. Then I would immediately turn it off. The cycle continued repeatedly.

Knowing my strong desire to complete the race, Zeke helped me get dressed again (which didn't make any sense to me). The rest of the crew and medical staff attempted to motivate me. "Come on, Russ. Get back out there and finish the race. You can do it." But I was dead set that I had finished Badwater hours ago. I couldn't figure out why I had to go and cross the finish line *again*.

I was so out of it that I told people I even built a house at the finish line and described it vividly. "It has a wraparound deck and everything. You can see all of Death Valley from up there," I told them.

I had gone completely off the deep end.

Despite this madness, my team returned to the stake in the ground that marked the pace where I had left the course. We resumed the race. (Event rules allow us to do this.)

After a half mile, the effort had become futile. With a pacer on both sides of me physically holding me up by my arms, I was losing it—in body, mind, and spirit. I forced the pacers away, laid back down on the road, and refused to move.

My crew did all they could. My race was over.

A few hours later, in the van ride back home, my mental fog lifted. I turned to Zeke and asked, "Did I not finish Badwater?"

"No, Russ. You didn't."

With that, I stared out the window and felt a wave of overwhelming disappointment. I had let everyone down.

My friends, my family, and I had made so many sacrifices. Now, it had been all for naught.

Looking back, I have a theory as to why I lost my mind: caffeine overdose. All the chemical stimulants, on top of my perilous physical condition in a dangerously sleep-deprived state, provided the perfect recipe for disaster.

I put far too much pressure on myself for that silly event. I took it way too seriously. It affected my sleep, which ended up being the deciding factor in my downfall for my first Badwater.

As a result of this epic experience, I've learned that people's negative reactions to adversity almost always make things worse. I now tell my kids (and anyone who will listen) that we can't control what happens in our lives, but we *can* control our reactions to them. One can choose to be stressed, angry, or sad, or one can choose to be chill, accepting, or happy. When I finally started applying this, I found it tremendously empowering.

Essentially, I've learned to chill the f*@k out!

Armed with a new attitude and some wisdom, I went on to cross the line at Badwater in my second attempt.

As terrible as the first experience was, I know there will always be another race. The first broke me down, but I came back stronger than ever.

TIPS AND TRICKS FOR USING P2D2 WHEN YOU DON'T CROSS THE FINISH LINE

Patience: Remind yourself that other opportunities will always arise, and in the meantime, you can work toward preparing yourself even more.

Persistence: Think of failures as learning opportunities. *Not* finishing Badwater taught me the consequences of putting too much pressure on myself to succeed.

Dedication: While I often tell people not to give up, to keep trying despite the pain, there comes a point when your efforts (and stubbornness) can become dangerous. Dedicate yourself to the big picture. No goal is worth death or destruction. Your health is always the priority.

Discipline: It takes discipline to try again after a devastating failure. Don't sit in your disappointment. Get back to work as soon as you can. Find a new goal and set your sights on it.

EXTREME GREATNESS CHALLENGE:

Take a few moments to think or journal about the following questions:

- What do you consider to be the biggest failure in your life?
- What did that failure teach you?
- How do you feel about the idea of failure, in general?

CHAPTER 6

EXTREME GREATNESS DOESN'T ALWAYS LOOK AS YOU THOUGHT IT WOULD

"Our greatest weakness lies in giving up. The most certain way to succeed is always to try just one more time."

—THOMAS EDISON

In the quest for Extreme Greatness, we plan, we prepare, we anticipate, we develop a support team…. Despite all of this, life can throw a curve ball. As you stand in the batter's box and see the ball wobbling toward you, you can either freak out (and strike out) or strengthen your grip on the bat and go for it. You can fall apart or be humble. You may not hit a home run, but you can still get on base.

The following story illustrates how dedication and persistence allowed me to succeed despite the curve balls. This story is "Death by a Thousand Pine Needles."

I'm embarrassed to share the ridiculousness of this race.

At mile 165, during the depths of night three at the Tahoe 200 Endurance Run, I was freezing my ass off. Exhausted, hungry, dehydrated, and sleep-deprived, I couldn't generate any body heat. Even though we were warned of lower temperatures, I had left the last checkpoint without enough warm clothes. At the current temp of 30°, my lightweight nylon windbreaker and running tights didn't come close to doing the job.

I tried to pick up my pace but couldn't because of my weakened condition. The harder I tried, the worse I felt. I curled into a tight ball under a tree and covered myself with dirt and leaves, hoping to warm up. It was futile. I didn't know what to do. If I carried on, I would be miserable. If I stopped, I would get colder.

I decided to keep walking as fast as I could muster, making slow forward progress to the next checkpoint, which was ten or fifteen miles up the trail. Going backward to the previous checkpoint was not a viable option for me.

In desperation, I wracked my brain for a way to warm myself. I was in the middle of a dense forest, surrounded by pine trees, and wondered if nature could assist.

"Aha! I'll just stuff pine branches between my shirts like a Halloween scarecrow."

I broke off small twigs and started stuffing away. After five minutes of this madness, I stopped, realizing the branches only served to jab against my shirt in all directions without giving any insulation.

Then, I thought, "Hey, how about just tons of pine needles?"

I pulled out the silly twigs and replaced them with endless handfuls of pine needles, packing them in so tightly that I looked like the Michelin Man.

Surprisingly, it worked. I wasn't an icicle anymore. The pine needles were keeping me warm, but they were also poking my skin uncomfortably. Much worse, they were sliding down into my private area. Some serious damage occurred with each step, forcing me to waddle like a penguin.

I had a decision to make—stay warm and get poked to death, or freeze and not get poked. I chose to stay warm and just deal with the circumstances later. My only hope was that I would see another runner who would be willing to lend me a layer of clothes.

After about an hour of feeling like my nether region was being devoured by fire ants, I saw the dancing light of a headlamp coming from behind me. My prayers might be answered!

The runner from Australia noticed immediately that I didn't look right. He laughed his ass off when he learned I had pine needles torturing me with each step. I begged him to lend me an extra shirt or jacket.

"Sure, mate," he said. "I've got this jacket that I rarely wear but always bring anyway. It's all yours."

He pulled out a medium-weight polyester shirt folded neatly into a labeled resealable bag. I couldn't believe his level of organization and preparation.

He pulled away from me as I did some "landscaping" by removing as many needles as possible. I wished at the time that I had a leaf blower.

With the extra clothing layer, I could feel the cold dissipate within ten minutes. I was back in action, thanks to my Aussie friend. I didn't catch his name, but to this day, I still remember his race number.

At the next checkpoint, the medical guys gave me lubricating lotion, but the damage had been done. Despite enduring a challenge that probably doesn't happen to ultrarunners very often, I was able to make it to the finish line in one piece.

The next day at the post-race awards dinner party, I recognized my Aussie friend talking amongst a group of people. I called out to him, "Hey, are you number 54?"

"Pine Needle Guy!" he replied.

All his Aussie friends burst out in laughter, obviously having been told the story by him.

We shared many good memories of the race, with my saga being the headliner.

It took me about a week to recover from my injuries.

The hilarity of this race taught me two important lessons. One, humor and humility are your friends in difficult circumstances. Two, low moments are the breeding ground for innovation (as long as you remain open to the fact that success may not look as you thought it would).

TIPS AND TRICKS FOR USING P2D2 WHEN FACING DOWN A CURVE BALL

Patience: Have self-compassion in low moments. Give yourself the grace to ask for help and to embrace the absurdity.

Persistence: Difficult circumstances call for a reassessment of priorities. Does it really matter how you reach your end goal?

Dedication: Be humbly in service of your goal, no matter how ridiculous you look.

Discipline: Take a moment to think about your definition of success. This clarity will keep you aligned with what you are striving for when things get complicated. My goal was not to finish the race looking strong, fit, and handsome. My goal was to finish at all costs.

Extreme Greatness Challenge:

Give yourself a score for each of the following traits:

1 - I don't possess this trait.

2 - I sometimes possess this trait.

3 - I embody this trait often.

- Humor

- Innovation

- The ability to pivot/think on my feet

- Humility

- Self-compassion

CHAPTER 7

YOU NEED TO BE BROKEN DOWN TO LEVEL UP

"Some people believe holding on and hanging in there are signs of great strength. However, there are times when it takes much more strength to know when to let go and then do it."

– ANN LANDERS

By now, you've probably come to the conclusion that achieving Extreme Greatness is a painful process, not for the faint of heart. You may even ask yourself if you are cut out for it, if the reward is worth the pain.

I can't answer that for you.

What I *can* tell you is that P2D2 has helped me embrace physical, emotional, mental, and spiritual strife and harness it in a way that has made me a better man. The difficulty, the pain, is exactly what has made me great.

Maybe this story about my hardest race ever will help you understand…

The question people ask me most often is, "Russ, why do you do those crazy ultras?"

I've previously shared that I don't have a simple answer to such a complicated question. Everyone walks away unfulfilled, expecting some insightful, compelling answer. My best answer to date is that I get great satisfaction from seeking self-improvement and from facing self-imposed challenges. I'm a person who must have a goal at all times. When I reach one, I set another. I crave the challenge of going further or surviving in worse conditions. Non-extreme athletes simply can't understand, but we don't need them to try. Ultrarunners do the sport for themselves only. *We* are our only competition.

The second most common question I face is, "What's the hardest race you've ever done?"

I've done some doozies, including the famous Badwater 135, Moab 240, and Tahoe 200. I've slept in -46° Fahrenheit temperatures in the Yukon of Canada. At the other end of the spectrum, I've raced in 128° Fahrenheit. But my greatest test was the 330-mile Iditarod Trail Invitational in Alaska. On the same course as the famous Iditarod Trail Sled Dog Race, this event requires near-total self-sufficiency in the most remote and harsh wilderness.

The conditions require racers to pull a sled of their own provisions. There is no van loaded with snacks and a soft, dry, and warm place to nap. We mostly sleep out on the trail (though we can sleep inside at some of the checkpoints). More than a marathon distance separates each of the checkpoints. We face mind-breaking isolation, bone-chilling cold, and penetrating winds.

I was confident I could finish despite having not completed a similar 300-mile race two times in Canada. I had made easily correctable mistakes—or so I thought.

A mere thirty miles into the event, I came upon another racer. We both had lost the tracks of others ahead of us. Following our GPS trackers, we knew we were going the right way. On the race path, we encountered chest-deep snow—even with snowshoes, we sank down to our chins. Every ten steps, the thick snow would rip a snowshoe off, and I would have to dig down with my hands to feel for it because I couldn't see it in the deep powder under the night sky.

Hiking poles didn't help, as the ground was too far below the snow to allow pushing off. We were left with no choice but to lean forward and effectively swim through the snow, dragging our sixty-pound sleds behind us. No joke, but it seemed like we were dragging a refrigerator. We still had 300 miles to go.

After an hour of this torture, and so early in the event, we questioned whether we were (pun intended) "in over our heads."

Left with no choice, we trudged on. Eventually, we found a snowmobile track that had packed the snow down, somewhat lessening the ordeal. We followed his path to a river, where the going became much easier.

Despite this small victory, the race "broke me" mentally at around mile 120. Sleep-deprived, cold, hungry, and without a shred of confidence left, I attempted to catch some sleep at the checkpoint.

Sleep can be elusive at these checkpoints. As much as I needed to, I couldn't doze off in this makeshift shelter, laying on a floor of hay amongst other loudly snoring racers. What I needed most eluded me, which was rest. Without sleep, I fell into a deep hole emotionally and decided to quit the race.

Simple yet so tremendously important, sleep, or lack thereof, can make or break one's performance in work and play. In extreme sports, we push and push right to the red line. It's so easy to hammer away the caffeine to forgo stopping, but eventually, we break down. Often, we go too far and enter a shock state that ironically prevents falling asleep despite being near total functional shutdown. I may fidget or have involuntary muscle contractions. My pounding heartbeat has kept me awake. Or, my body aches so much that I can't get comfortable. You might remember from my Badwater race that this problem can take an athlete out of the race.

Here I was again, dancing with the devil of insomnia. I couldn't keep myself from obsessing over how much farther I had to go and thus trapped myself in a dooming negative mindset. I couldn't escape from the thought that I just wasn't tough enough to do these stupid races. I cycled through ridiculous excuses such as *I'm too old for this*.

In a fit of tremendous mental weakness, I told a race official, "I'm done."

Luckily, he knew me from other races and asked, "Russ, are you SURE?"

"Yes. Can I take the plane back in the morning?"

He blew me off, having seen countless others succumb to this mindset in the depths of the "pain cave" of ultras. But my mind was made up. After getting sleep, other fortunate athletes would return to the trail. I would not.

I tossed and turned, and miraculously, I must have slept. It was a gift from God because in my slumber, my mental state had cleared. I told myself that I wasn't a pathetic wussy and that I was strong enough to compete out here. I dug deep into my soul and flipped my psyche 180 degrees.

"F*@k it," I shouted.

At that moment, I made the choice to replace all of my negative thinking with positive thinking. As I gathered my supplies, a friend I had met on the trail told me he was heading out. I went with him. I was back in the game!

Within a few hours, I rose from one of my lowest states ever and found the strength to continue. Changing my mental state was a win, but I still had a lot of work to do.

After a while, my friend pulled away from me such that I raced basically alone for the next nearly 150 miles, except for brief periods of meeting other racers on the trail. It was grueling, but I kept trying to celebrate small victories along the way. When I reached the turnaround point, my spirits soared. I had completed more than half the race. "It's all downhill from here," I told myself.

Uh, not really.

At mile 200, something terrible happened. I had a little accident. Coming down a long, exposed slope, nature called, and she called fast. I made a mess in my pants. I didn't have time to get into my sled bag for "supplies."

I knew I couldn't do the rest of the race like this, and certainly not in these frigid, arctic conditions. I had no choice but to clean myself with snow…using my hands. After each wipe, I would clean my hands with fresh snow. I worked as fast as I could, trying to warm them up as much as possible in between passes. Totally exposed in -20° temperatures with twenty-mph winds, this was cruel and unusual punishment. I honestly couldn't believe this was happening to me.

After ten minutes of frantic "housecleaning," I used up all the clean snow in a ten-foot-wide radius. The area looked like a moose had been killed by a pack of wolves. I can't imagine what the next racer thought when they came along the scene.

I carried on. Three hours later, I came to a lodge where I could change into my backup clothes and, as a bonus, get out of these dreadful conditions. I was as good as new. Or so I told myself.

I amped myself up for what would be a tough sixty-mile section to the next checkpoint. My plan: attack, attack, attack. Using up all my caffeine, I charged and made good time, passing a few racers ahead of me. Along the way, some buffalo hunters offered me some moose sausage. Some Alaska State Troopers out on routine patrol gave me a few Diet Cokes. I kept finding small blessings, and gratitude kept me going.

I slept out on the trail a few times. Once I dug a snow cave under a fallen tree, experiencing some of the most serene moments of my life. Another time, I slept only three feet off the trail and was awakened by the sounds of an Iditarod dog musher swooshing by, led by eight pairs of eyes reflecting toward me. (These breathtaking and surreal moments are additional reasons I do ultramarathons.) By the final checkpoint, I had caught up with several friends/fellow racers. They thought I had dropped out and couldn't believe I had risen from the ashes. (Neither could I.)

We slept a solid four hours. The plan was to get a good rest and then power the last forty miles to the finish. But the tolls of having not slept enough earlier coupled with the rigors of the previous 290 miles caught up to me. I had reached my limit. Caffeine no longer had any effect. The "horse" was being whipped repeatedly, but it wouldn't budge.

I couldn't stand up any longer. My mental will was broken. I HAD TO STOP.

Only seven miles from the finish, I simply couldn't stay awake. I hated to succumb to exhaustion so close to the finish, but I had no choice. I wouldn't have made it any further without sleeping. I stayed in the tent, dressed fully in my clothes with my boots sticking out. I risked frostbite on my feet, but at this point, I didn't care.

When I woke up three hours later, my tent and sled were covered in eight inches of snow. I swallowed caffeinated energy powder straight—without water—and was invigorated enough for the final push to victory lane.

In the end, I made it.

This race almost broke me. In fact, I gave in to my negativity more than once. If it hadn't been for years of P2D2 training, I would never have made it to the finish line.

In times when you feel broken down to the core, just remember that the moment will pass. You can build yourself up again and continue on the journey. It's possible. Trust me.

TIPS AND TRICKS FOR USING P2D2 WHEN YOU ARE ON THE VERGE OF GIVING UP

Patience: Moments of desperation pass, and if we have the patience to stay focused on the goal, chances are you will be able to reinvigorate your energy and drive.

Persistence: Embrace the suck! Sometimes, there is nothing you can do but acknowledge the adversity and keep moving forward.

Dedication: When your confidence is shaken, remember why you got out of bed this morning.

Discipline: Continually remind yourself that you are your only competition. Other competitors likely finished the race stronger and faster than me, but I fought my own battle and won on my terms.

EXTREME GREATNESS CHALLENGE:

When things downright suck, we usually fall into our default mode.

Which one of the four pillars do you usually default to in difficult circumstances?

Which one of these pillars are you least likely to default to?

Developing an awareness of your strengths and stretches is valuable when the going gets tough. While we rely on our strengths, it is equally important to build up our capacity in the pillars we don't utilize. Ideally, you want a full toolbox!

CHAPTER 8

WHEN IT ALL COMES TOGETHER

"You may encounter many defeats, but you must not be defeated. In fact, it may be necessary to encounter the defeats so you can know who you are, what you can rise from, how you can still come out of it."

– MAYA ANGELOU

The sweetest victories take time and endurance. They rely on every ounce of P2D2 that lives within you. As I share the following story about one of the most challenging and exhilarating races of my life, I want you to know that while it was an incredible success, it wasn't easy.

Extreme Greatness is never easy. Nor does it come quickly. It is the journey of a lifetime.

Most people thought I was truly crazy when they learned I was attempting the full-distance 430-mile event of the Yukon Arctic Ultra after having not finished the 300-mile distance three times previously.

I didn't care what they thought. This was my year.

I had prepared perfectly and couldn't have been more physically fit or stronger. Mentally, I felt as ready as I could be. Kit-wise and logistically, I had zero concerns, and the cold didn't scare me.

I told myself to stay in the moment, break the race down into small segments, and don't think about the magnitude of 430 miles.

A six-mile test on the Yukon River of my new sled and gear a few days before the event reinforced my confidence.

At the start, I could barely contain my energy. I settled into a brisk walking pace, feeling like the journey would be effortless, despite dragging my sixty-five-pound sled, packed with spare clothes, hot water, a shovel, a hatchet, spare batteries and power banks, headlamps, an emergency satellite phone, a stove, a -60° sleeping bag, a bivy sack, a foot care kit, and enough food to feed a small village.

I arrived at the first checkpoint earlier than expected but feeling fantastic—no sweating, overheating, or foot issues.

After a quick meal and the required frostbite check from the medics, I headed out toward Dog Grave Lake, which was designated as Checkpoint #2.

I made it to Dog Grave Lake without any problems, unlike the previous year when I had all kinds of silly issues. Along the Takhini River, I returned to my brisk pace and shared some enjoyable miles with my Spanish friend, Kike Maravilla—a multi-time non-finisher who, like me, was determined to make it to Dawson this year.

Halfway to Checkpoint #3 at Braeburn, I tried to take a couple-hour nap but couldn't fall asleep. I decided to just get up and get going. While getting organized to set out again, I noted my heart was pounding and racing in the low 100's at rest. I hadn't had any caffeine yet, so I was perplexed and frustrated by this.

I left Braeburn with John Nakel, an engineer from Ohio. We ended up working together the entire next fifty-two-mile segment to Mandana Lake, Checkpoint #4.

Sleep eluded both of us there. The brilliant sunshine made it hard, despite us covering our eyes. Additionally, we both hated to sleep during the coveted daytime hours. Again, we decided to just carry on.

John and I trudged to Carmacks, Checkpoint #5, where I was finally able to get about four hours of decent sleep. Robert, the Race Director, mentioned that he was 100% positive I would finish the race this year. I appreciated his confidence, but I must admit it did put some extra pressure on me.

I left Carmacks with two Danish studs, Henrik and Michael, but I couldn't keep up with their pace, so I reminded myself to run my own race. We leapfrogged often when they would stop for feeds. I also shared some miles with a Canadian, Brian James.

I fought off the torturous sleep monster and finally made it to Checkpoint #6, McCabe. I was exhausted and looking forward to a rest. There, I met Joel Rennie from Australia, the bloke who I would end up doing the rest of the race with. Joel introduced himself after seeing me attempting to treat my blisters and offered to provide his ER nursing skills. As we chatted, I learned how Joel got sick the night before the race. Despite a warrior mentality, he had a lengthy stop at the first checkpoint to recover. With the race director's approval, he reentered the race at Carmacks, hoping to salvage his experience, now as an "unranked" participant. Joel had come all the way from Australia, trained very hard, paid a ton of money, and brought his girlfriend and parents with him. He was determined to cross the finish line.

After a few minutes of chatting and treating my blisters, Joel remarked, "Russ, I think I'll head out with you."

We got along great and worked very well together. I'm grateful for his help and to have shared so many miles together.

I still felt stronger each day as my sleep improved. Other than periods of severe back and thoracic wall pain, my body gave me no issues. I attributed it to wearing my fairly heavy three-liter hydration bladder.

Joel and I made it to Checkpoint #7, Pelly Crossing, and I felt great physically. Though the area was a little cramped and busy, I was able to rest in preparation for the next thirty-two-mile section down the Pelly River to Pelly Farm. On the river, we were treated to a glorious Aurora Borealis/Northern Lights show. We slept a few hours in -25° temps.

The next morning, I awoke to experience a wonderful moment where I finally felt certain I would finish the race. This belief empowered me.

At Pelly Farm, Checkpoint #8, the athletes were treated like family. Our hosts, the Bradleys, offered tons of food, and I devoured as many calories as possible. I also got my first deep, high-quality sleep.

We headed out for a dreaded sixty-five-mile unsupported section of the race toward Checkpoint #9, Indian River. Along the way, I told myself that this was my "race within the race." If I could survive this, I had the race in the bag.

At Pelly, we had learned that the Scroggie Creek Checkpoint was moved nineteen miles further, meaning we would have another sixty-nine-mile section awaiting us. This realization crushed me but didn't break me. This is the moment I had prepared for. I told myself to attack it in two-hour sections, hoping to take off five- or seven-mile chunks at a time. I knew when we got to the checkpoint, we would "only" have a thirty-one-mile, mostly downhill jaunt into the finish.

With dogged patience and persistence, Joel and I made it to both checkpoints.

Our spirits were sky high leaving the last checkpoint, knowing we had one last climb up the famed "King Solomon's Dome" and then a steady downhill into Dawson City.

I felt like I could run ten-minute miles easily. I encountered some "GI distress" along the way that forced me to stop frequently, but I soldiered on, appreciating Joel's patience.

Euphoria building with each step closer, I felt as if I were running without my sled. I had been pulling away from Joel without even trying. Earlier, I asked him about how we should handle the finish line. He told me to go ahead and cross by myself. Not at peace with his answer, considering how much he had helped me, and based on how we had bonded over so many miles, I pushed him to stay with me.

We met Jessie Howland on the river outside town, and she told us there were only four kilometers left. While her intentions were to share words of motivation, I thought the finish was just a few hundred meters away, so I was overcome with disappointment. Knowing how important mindset is, I told myself to savor the last few miles, which I most assuredly did.

A little later, I caught a glimpse of the finish line on Front Street in Dawson. Could it be? Was I truly finishing this thing? It didn't seem real.

I can't describe the sheer satisfaction and unadulterated euphoria in finishing that race. I had achieved a huge goal after having been defeated three times previously in the shorter 300-mile distance. I wasn't trying to prove anything to anyone. It wasn't about revenge or vindication. I had challenged myself and myself only. I accomplished my goal after making lots of sacrifices, enduring tremendous amounts of discomfort and delayed gratification. To be blunt, I was super f*@king proud of myself.

My success was not despite my previous failures but *because* of them. Each time I struggled and didn't finish a race, I built up my P2D2 muscles, becoming mentally and physically stronger. Everything I had experienced previously led to this exact moment when I was able to achieve Extreme Greatness.

EXTREME GREATNESS CHALLENGE:

In our quest for Extreme Greatness, it is important to stop from time to time and look back—see how far you've come.

List two or three epic wins you've had over the last six to twelve months.

Did you stop to celebrate them?

LIFE IS NOT A SPRINT. IT'S AN ULTRAMARATHON.

Like racing, the journey toward Extreme Greatness is a lifelong quest. The journey will have highs and lows, triumphs and setbacks, even moments that feel impossible. Being patient, persistent, dedicated, and disciplined is not a box you check because you have learned enough, grown enough. The finish line comes on your deathbed when you can look back on your life with pride and gratitude.

P2D2 does not make you immune to life's devastation, but perhaps provides you with tools to cultivate resilience. Though I have sunk into the dark depths during some of my races, it was nothing compared to the utter despair of learning of my brother's death after being struck by a truck on a cross-country bicycle trip, or the sadness of having to say goodbye to my father who was losing his battle with colon cancer.

In the lowest times, I found gratitude for the love I shared with those I've lost.

I truly believe human beings can get through anything life throws at us. We have the potential not only to survive, but to rise above and discover new potential.

If you take only one thing away from reading this book, I want you to remember this: don't ever give up on chasing your goals.

I don't define failure by the goals I reached for but never achieved. To me, failure is giving up on chasing my goals or never going for it in the first place.

If you believe it's possible to achieve a goal, you probably can. First, one has to make the decision to set it. Then, make a plan. Finally, one has to work toward it. The most important step is <u>choosing</u> to go for it.

The individual is the greatest <u>limiter</u> of their own success. Moreso, the individual is the greatest <u>asset</u> leading to that success.

Don't settle.

Work toward having no regrets!

I love training. I love being fit. I love being outside. But mostly, I love inspiring others. I'm just an average guy with average abilities. The difference is, I have above-average drive and discipline. If I can do it, you can too.

> "With focused and unrelenting drive, I will strive to maximize my athletic potential while demonstrating to others, through example, the value of proper behavior, self-sacrifice, and discipline."
>
> – RUSS REINBOLT

WHAT IS YOUR EXTREME GREATNESS GRADE?

Answer these ten questions as honestly as possible on a 0 to 10 scale. 10 is the highest score, and 0 is the lowest.

To chase and achieve your Personal Greatness...

- How willing are you to sacrifice sleep?
- How willing are you to experience physical pain?
- How willing are you to delay gratification?
- How well do you tolerate obstacles and disappointment?
- How willing are you to do what others don't?
- How willing are you to work when others aren't watching?
- How well can you block out other people's negativity?
- How well can you control your emotions?

- How resilient are you? In other words, how big is your "Fight Factor"?
- How hard is it for you to be "broken"?

Add for total score.

A: 90-100 You WILL do it! You WILL accomplish your Personal Greatness or achieve your goal!

B: 80-89 You CAN do it. You CAN accomplish your Personal Greatness or achieve your goal.

C: 70-79 To be blunt, you probably won't make it. Honestly reassess your strengths and weaknesses, your goal, and your true reasons for trying.

D: <70 Help others chase their Greatness until you are ready to chase your own. Timing is everything. Your time will come. You have your entire life to begin the pursuit. Just don't wait until it's too late! Later, when you score above 80, "flip the switch" and frickin' GO FOR IT.

ACKNOWLEDGMENTS

I don't know where to begin when making a list of all those individuals who have helped me in my life and who continue to support my mission to achieve Extreme Greatness. My two older brothers, Jake and Alan, probably have had the greatest influence on me.

My parents, Nancy and Dale, sacrificed to no end to provide the best foundation a kid could have for a wonderful adult life.

I wish I could thank the innumerable teachers, coaches, and role models I've had. Many will never know they had such a beautiful and powerful impact on me.

Thank you to my good friend and advisor, Heather Hastey, for all she does for me but, most importantly, for bugging me to no end to actually start writing this book!

To my lovely wife, Diane, for her patience in putting up with a "crazy" husband. Though she admits to not understanding me, she supports me fully.

I am forever grateful to Krista Clive-Smith, Kel Cleeve, Ashley, Emma, and Makena at Empire Thought Leadership and Merack Publishing and Stephanie Clarke at Clarke International for their invaluable work on getting this project to the finish line.

ABOUT THE AUTHOR

After working in a busy San Diego, California, emergency department for nearly twenty-one years, Dr. Russ Reinbolt now travels to smaller ERs in the Pacific Northwest, caring for those in more rural communities.

A hit at parties, he has endless entertaining stories to tell after having served more than 100,000 patients to date.

Thirteen years ago, he completed his first ultramarathon. Dr. Russ started running in high school and hasn't stopped yet. Triathlons and road races were the foundation of his athletic life, leading to ever-more demanding events. He thrives on ultra-distance races in the most extreme environments, whether they be blazing hot or frigidly cold and remote.

He lives in San Diego with his wife of nineteen years, Diane, and his two teenage daughters.

Fun but dirty fact: Dr. Russ eats a 1,000-calorie bowl of ice cream before bed three nights a week!

Printed in the USA
CPSIA information can be obtained
at www.ICGtesting.com
CBHW021219201223
2791CB00003B/6